Eat Your Colors

Orange
Food
Fun

by Lisa Bullard

Capstone
press

Mankato, Minnesota

A+ Books are published by Capstone Press,
151 Good Counsel Drive, P.O. Box 669, Mankato, Minnesota 56002.
www.capstonepress.com

1 2 3 4 5 6 11 10 09 08 07 06

Library of Congress Cataloging-in-Publication Data
Bullard, Lisa.
  Orange food fun / Lisa Bullard.
    p. cm. — (A+ books. Eat your colors)
    Includes bibliographical references and index.
    ISBN-13: 978-0-7368-5382-8 (hardcover)
    ISBN-10: 0-7368-5382-0 (hardcover)
    1. Food—Juvenile literature. 2. Orange (Color)—Juvenile literature. I. Title. II. Series.
  TX355.B928 2006
  641.3—dc22   2005025836

Summary: Brief text and colorful photos describe common foods that are the color orange.

Credits

Erika L. Shores, editor; Kia Adams, designer; Kelly Garvin, photo researcher

Photo Credits

Capstone Press/Karon Dubke, all

Note to Parents, Teachers, and Librarians

This Eat Your Colors book uses full-color photographs and a nonfiction format to introduce children to the color orange. *Orange Food Fun* is designed to be read aloud to a pre-reader or to be read independently by an early reader. Photographs help listeners and early readers understand the text and concepts discussed. The book encourages further learning by including the following sections: Recipe, Glossary, Read More, Internet Sites, and Index. Early readers may need assistance using these features.

Table of Contents

Orange Food Fun

Chewy, gooey, fresh, and juicy. Orange foods make tasty treats. What is your favorite orange food?

Chomp, crunch, or chew those carrots! When the tops are bright green, these orange roots are ready to eat.

8

Scoop out the seeds
and squishy insides of a
butternut squash. Only
the orange flesh of this
vegetable is good to eat.

Cold Orange Foods

Squeezing oranges makes a tasty drink. An orange is a fruit with a name to match its color.

Quick, lick it before it drips! A frozen orange juice bar cools you down on a hot day.

Fruity, sweet, and creamy. Cold orange sherbet melts in your mouth.

Sweet Orange Foods

Peach slices are sweet.
This orange-colored fruit
has soft, fuzzy skin.

Meet the peach's little cousin. Orange apricots taste just as sweet but ripen earlier.

Bright orange pumpkins
baked with sugar and
spices turn into pumpkin pie.
This tasty pie is a favorite
Thanksgiving dessert.

21

Cheesy Orange Foods

Mice like to eat cheddar cheese. How about you? Do you nibble on this orange dairy food?

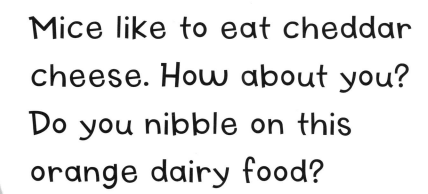

Spoon up a big bite of macaroni and cheese. Creamy cheese makes this gooey orange dish delicious.

Cheese puff snacks are made of corn and cheddar cheese. The orange color lasts long after the last crunchy bite.

Simple Orange Smoothie

You can create a tasty smoothie treat made with sweet orange ingredients.

What You Will Need

Measuring cups

Blender

Glass

½ cup (120 mL)
orange juice

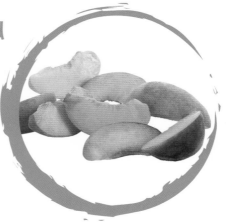

1 peach cut
into slices, or
1 cup (240 mL)
canned
peach slices

3 ice cubes

How to Make an Orange Smoothie

1. Have an adult help you cut up the fruit and use the blender.

2. Put the orange juice in the blender first, and then add the remaining ingredients.

3. Blend until smooth. Pour your smoothie into a glass. Drink and enjoy!

   Adding more yogurt will make your smoothie creamier. More ice cubes will make the smoothie thicker. You can add more orange juice to make the smoothie sweeter.

1 small container
of yogurt

29

Glossary

apricot (AP-ri-kot)—a small, soft fruit with a fuzzy orange skin; apricots have a sweet, tart taste.

root (ROOT)—the part of a plant that grows underground; roots bring water into plants.

sherbet (SHUR-buht)—a frozen dessert made of fruit juices, water, sugar, and milk

Read More

Schuette, Sarah L. *Orange*. Colors. Mankato, Minn.: Capstone Press, 2003.

Whitehouse, Patricia. *Orange Foods*. The Colors We Eat. Chicago: Heinemann, 2004.

Internet Sites

FactHound offers a safe, fun way to find Internet sites related to this book. All of the sites on FactHound have been researched by our staff.

Here's how:

1. Visit *www.facthound.com*

2. Type in this special code 0736853820 for age-appropriate sites. Or enter a search word related to this book for a more general search.

3. Click on the Fetch It button.

FactHound will fetch the best sites for you!

Index